POLAR BEARS

POLAR BEARS

NORBERT ROSING

FIREFLY BOOKS

A FIREFLY BOOK

Published by Firefly Books Ltd. 2010
Copyright © 2010 Norbert Rosing

First Printing

Publisher Cataloging-in-Publication Data (U.S.)
Rosing, Norbert.
    Polar bears / Norbert Rosing.
[   ] p. : col. photos. ; cm.
Includes index.
Summary: Photographs and captions present the life of polar bears across
the four seasons of the year. Topics covered include habitat, activities,
diet, anatomy, and survival.
ISBN-13: 978-1-55407-599-7 (bound)   ISBN-10: 1-55407-599-8 (bound)
ISBN-13: 978-1-55407-623-9 (pbk.)   ISBN-10: 1-55407-623-4 (pbk.)
1. Polar bear – Juvenile literature.   I. Title.
599.786 dc22   QL737.C27.R67 2010

Library and Archives Canada Cataloguing in Publication
Rosing, Norbert
    Polar bears / Norbert Rosing.
Includes index.
ISBN-13: 978-1-55407-599-7 (bound)   ISBN-10: 1-55407-599-8 (bound)
ISBN-13: 978-1-55407-623-9 (pbk.)   ISBN-10: 1-55407-623-4 (pbk.)
1. Polar bear--Juvenile literature. I. Title.
QL737.C27R663 2009   j599.786   C2009-905798-0

Published in the United States by
Firefly Books (U.S.) Inc.
P.O. Box 1338, Ellicott Station
Buffalo, New York 14205

Published in Canada by
Firefly Books Ltd.
66 Leek Crescent
Richmond Hill, Ontario L4B 1H1

Front cover design: Sari Naworynski

Manufactured by Printplus Limited in Shen Zhen, Guang Dong,
P.R.China in December, 2009, Job #S091100295.

The publisher gratefully acknowledges the financial support for our
publishing program by the Government of Canada through the Canada
Book Fund as administered by the Department of Canadian Heritage.

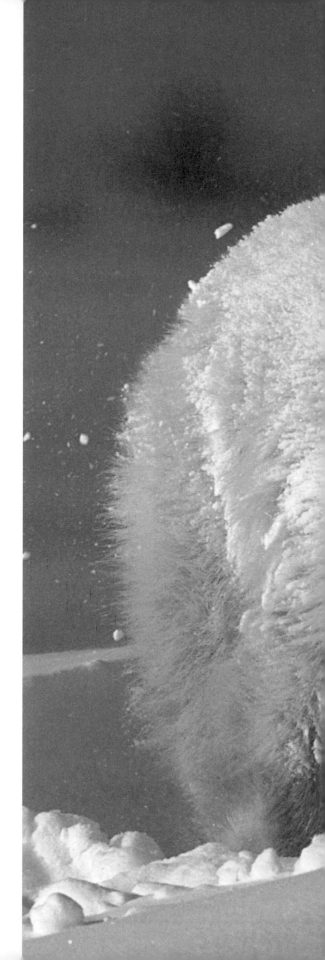

CONTENTS

INTRODUCTION

Bears have captured the human imagination for thousands of years. One of the most spectacular species is the polar bear—the largest land predator on Earth. Polar bears are famous for their brilliant white coats. Yet although it appears white, the fur is actually transparent, and each hair is hollow.

Male polar bears weigh between 550 and 1,700 pounds (250–770 kg) and are usually about 8 to 10 feet tall (2.5–3 m). Females weigh less than half that amount and are usually between 6 and 8 feet tall (1.8–2.5 m). About 20,000–25,000 polar bears live in the world's five "polar bear nations": Canada, the United States (Alaska), Russia, Denmark (Greenland) and Norway.

Scientists believe that the polar bear's ancestors were a group of brown bears isolated by glaciers off the coast of Siberia over 200,000 years ago. They slowly adapted to their harsh surroundings and evolved into the creatures we know today.

Thousands of people travel to the Arctic every year to watch polar bears. The size and strength of the bears, as well as their playfulness and beauty, endear them to us. Polar bears are curious creatures and will wrestle with each other, play with local dogs, explore garbage dumps or make their own fun with an old tire.

This book begins with the cub's early days—the den, and then the curious first days outside it. It then looks at how the polar bear adapts to its environment—swimming, making the journey to sea ice and searching for food. Next is an introduction to some of the bear's Arctic neighbors, including seals, arctic foxes, beluga whales and caribou. The book ends with a look at the bear in its landscape—fighting the elements, and then taking time for rest and recreation.

Today, polar bears are at great risk. The polar bear nations have signed agreements to protect this species. If current warming trends continue in the Arctic, however, two-thirds of the world's polar bear population could disappear by 2050. It is tragic that we are in danger of losing such a magnificent and powerful animal.

EARLY DAYS

The entrance tunnel to a den is usually about 6 feet (2 m) long but only about 2 feet (60 cm) wide. That's a tight squeeze for a full-grown bear.

Most polar bear dens are a single room—about 6 by 10 feet (2 x 3 m) in area and 4 feet (1.2 m) high. Here a mother is rolling in the snow to clean herself while her cub stares at the outside world for the first time.

above
After emerging from the darkness of the den in late March or
April, cubs take advantage of the long hours of sun. The sun
is an important heat source for young cubs, who still must
develop a thick layer of fat.

right
Polar bear mothers stay with their cubs when they first emerge
from the den. When bear cubs stumble from the den, they
already weigh at least 22 pounds (10 kg). They will need to
nurse for at least another 18 months.

This mother polar bear was resting on the tundra, and her cub was playing on her back. Then she suddenly decided to stand up. The cub didn't want to let go, so mom gave junior a short ride on her back.

When cubs are born they weigh less than 2 pounds (1 kg), but they quickly gain weight by drinking their mother's milk. This milk has a very high fat content—over 30 percent. The milk sold at the grocery store has a fat content of only 2 or 3 percent.

These cubs are about three months old and have been out of the den for about one week. During this time, mother polar bears rarely let their cubs out of their sight. If a cub strays too far, the mother makes a noisy puffing sound (called chuffing). Play-fighting can be fun. It also teaches essential survival skills that the cubs will soon need.

right
This photo of a cub giving a "high-five" to its mother is the result of many hours spent in the bitter cold by the photographer.

About two weeks after emerging from the den, the mother polar bear begins a journey to the sea ice, followed by her cubs. During the time in the den, the mother did not eat or drink. Her fat deposits are now almost gone.

During their journey, a mother bear often pulls her cubs over high snowbanks. The long days of walking can be exhausting for cubs. Many do not survive their first year.

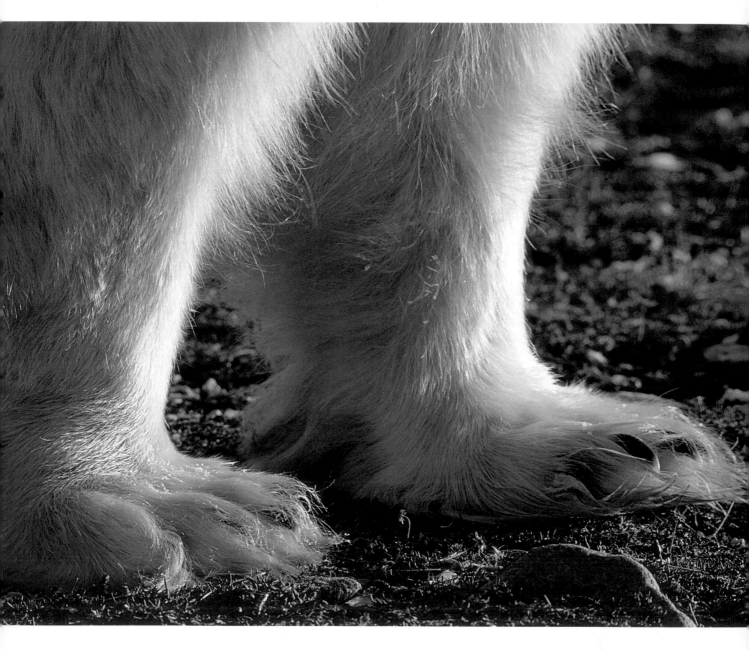

With its long claws, a polar bear can pull a 600-pound
(270 kg) seal out of its breathing hole.

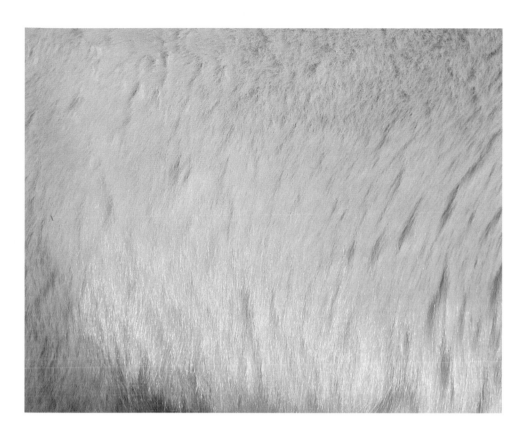

This is a close-up photograph of polar bear fur. A polar bear's coat consists of three layers: dense fur, skin and fat.

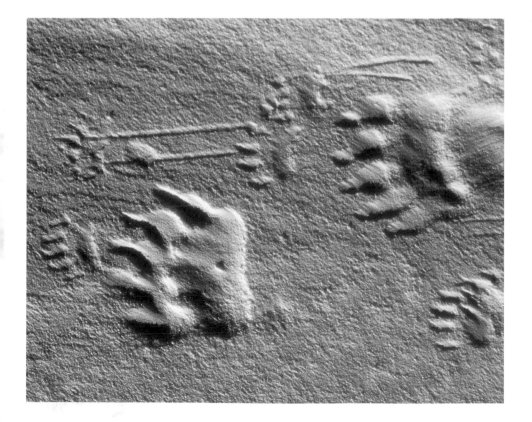

These footprints are from a female polar bear and her three-month-old cub.

Polar bears are excellent swimmers and have been known to swim up to six miles (10 km) an hour and as far as 60 miles (100 km) at a stretch. The bears paddle with their front feet and steer with their back feet.

Polar bears often over-
heat. Sometimes they
venture into the waters
just to cool off. When
a bear climbs on an
ice floe, it shakes itself
off—preventing ice from
forming on its fur.

This polar bear is not trying to walk on his hind legs—he's pouncing on a mouse that's traveling in tunnels beneath the snow. Polar bears are often forced to hunt for tiny rodents when food runs short in the summer and fall months.

above
This polar bear is trying to invite himself to dinner at a research camp. Hunger often forces animals into contact with humans. This contact can sometimes be deadly.

next page
Polar bears roam far out onto the sea ice in search of a seal's breathing hole.

We usually see photographs of polar bears with a brilliant
snowy background and forget that summer comes to the
Arctic, too. Here, a bear makes his way to a whale carcass that
has washed up on shore.

A polar bear emerges from the ocean and sneaks up to a walrus herd.

The walruses are now aware of the polar bear. They begin stampeding into the water as the bear looks for his prey. Attacking such a huge, dangerous animal is a last resort for a hungry polar bear.

ARCTIC NEIGHBORS

above
To keep the breathing hole open, a harp seal mother uses her claws to widen the opening in the sea ice.

right
The polar bear's spring diet of seal pups provides most of the needed calories for the year. Here, a harp seal pup wakes up after a snowstorm.

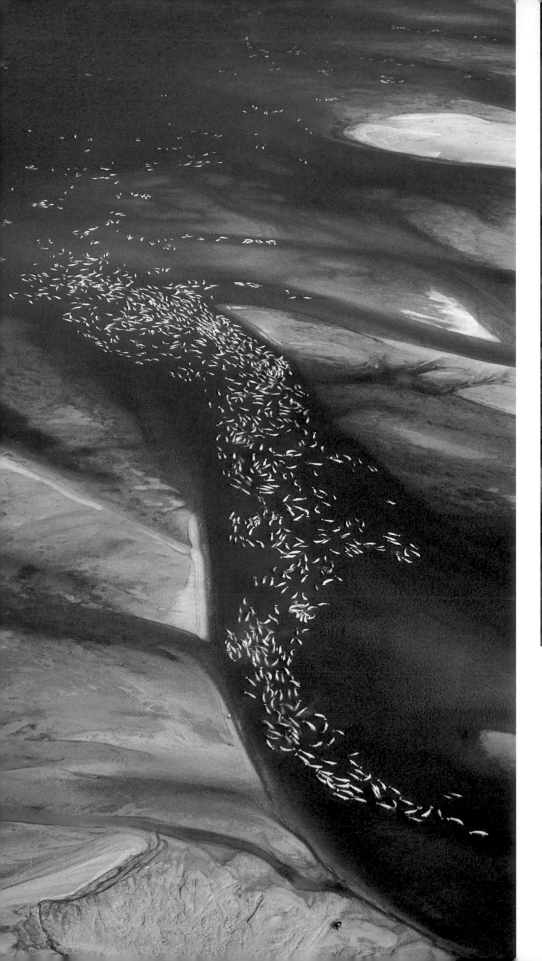

above
Beluga whales weigh between 2,000 and 3,000 pounds
(900–1,300 kg) and are between 13 and 20 feet (4–6 m) long.
They sometimes provide a food source for hungry polar bears.

left
In July, beluga whales gather in Cunningham Inlet in the
Canadian Arctic. They drift into the river to give birth.

A walrus cow and her newborn calf rest on a tiny ice floe in
the Arctic. Mothers must constantly watch their young, who
are easy prey for hungry polar bears. Adult walruses, however,
are rarely attacked because of their huge size.

A full-grown adult male walrus, such as this one, weighs about 2,800 pounds (1,300 kg). Walruses are at home in the water and are able to swim up to 12 miles (20 km) an hour.

above
Caribou travel for great distances in large herds. In winter, they live in forests on the edge of the Arctic.

right
The arctic fox is a Northern scavenger that frequently trails polar bears to eat the leftovers. Polar bears usually tolerate their tiny shadows. But if a fox gets too close, a bear will give it a swift swat of a paw.

above
These six-week-old arctic fox pups are waiting for their father to
bring back lemmings for dinner. A single family of arctic foxes
can eat as many as 4,000 lemmings during the breeding season.

right
An arctic fox crosses the frozen Churchill River in the Canadian
Arctic.

Muskoxen are distant relatives of sheep and goats. They have thick coats that hang down to the ground. When the adults feel threatened, they gather into a tight circle around their calves.

In winter, the arctic hare's thick coat becomes white to blend with the snow. In summer, it turns a gray-brown color.

A group of young ground squirrels play outside an entrance to their burrow.

At Home in the Arctic

above
In August, the Arctic becomes quieter. Summer visitors have left before the return of the bitter cold. Caribou herds, flocks of geese and other animals begin migrating south. Polar bears begin their own migration north to meet the coming ice and snow.

right
A polar bear rests under a piece of driftwood along the coastline of Canada's Wapusk National Park. Visitors to the park can observe polar bears in their native surroundings. "Wapusk" is the Cree word for "white bear." The park protects one of the world's largest known polar bear denning areas.

Strong winds change the shapes of snowdrifts. A snowdrift is much denser than freshly fallen snow. On extremely cold or stormy days, polar bears hollow out shelters in snowdrifts.

This sleepy-looking polar bear is slowly being covered with snow. As the snow drifts around the bear, it provides insulation and shelter.

above
On very cold days, polar bears will sometimes curl up together for warmth. They put their back to the wind, cover their muzzle and let the snow drift around them for better protection.

left
While his cousins to the south are sleeping the winter away, this polar bear is at his most active. During the fall and winter months, only pregnant females enter a den.

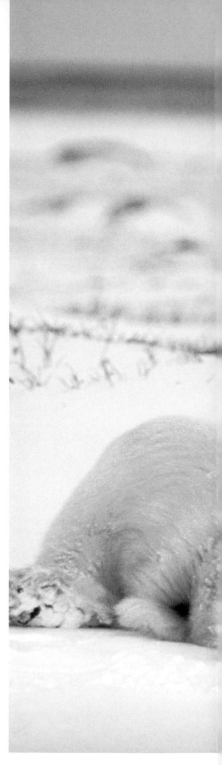

Polar bears are known to approach sled dogs and play with them. Usually both animals enjoy themselves, but if the animals get too excited, the large polar bear can easily kill his playmate.

While he waited for ice to form on Hudson Bay, this bear found an old tire on the tundra and turned it into a toy.

above
This was the first time the photographer had ever seen polar bears wrestling on a lake in the middle of a snowstorm. Play-fighting among polar bears is usually harmless.

right
This bear was sleeping in a snowbank. Then he began to do his morning execises, getting ready for another day in the cold.

POLAR BEAR FACTS

The polar bear is the largest land predator alive today. Its scientific name is *Ursus maritimus*, which means "sea bear."

HOW MANY POLAR BEARS ARE THERE, AND WHERE DO THEY LIVE?

Today, there are about 20,000 to 25,000 polar bears that roam the Arctic. Polar bears live in the circumpolar North in five "polar bear nations": Canada, the United States (Alaska), Russia, Denmark (Greenland) and Norway. Polar bears—or evidence of their presence—have been found nearly as far north as the Pole.

HOW BIG ARE THEY?

Adult males (boars) measure between 8 and 10 feet tall (2.5–3 m). They weigh 550 to 1,700 pounds (250–770 kg). Adult females (sows) measure 6 to 8 feet tall (1.8–2.5 m) and weigh 200 to 700 pounds (90–320 kg).

WHAT ABOUT CUBS?

Cubs are born in snow dens, in November or December. Cubs are usually born in pairs and weigh about 16 to 24 ounces (450–680 g). Cubs are blind and deaf for the first few weeks of life. When the mother and cubs emerge from the den in late March or April, the cubs weigh about 22–33 pounds (10–15 kg). Cubs usually stay with their mother until they are about two-and-a-half years old.

WHAT IS THE POLAR BEAR'S DIET?

Seals are their favorite food. Polar bears sometimes kill and eat walruses and beluga whales. Depending on how hungry they are, they will also eat land mammals, waterfowl, fish and vegetation. A polar bear has 42 teeth.

WHEN DO POLAR BEARS BREED?

Females breed only once every three years, during April and May. They have their first set of cubs between the ages of four and eight years.

WHAT IS THEIR LIFE SPAN?

Adult females in the wild live into their late 20s. Adult males in the wild live into their late teens or early 20s.

DO POLAR BEARS HIBERNATE?

Polar bears do not hibernate in the true sense of the word—they undergo a "walking hibernation." During the fall and winter months, only pregnant female bears enter a den.

How sharp are their senses?

A polar bear's hearing and sight are as sensitive as a human's. Polar bears have an excellent sense of smell. They can locate seals up to 20 miles (32 km) away.

What about their fur and skin?

A polar bear appears white because each hair—which is really a clear, hollow tube—reflects light. A polar bear's coat consists of dense fur, a layer of blubber and black skin.

What about their paws and limbs?

Polar bears have wide front paws with slightly webbed toes. They paddle with their front feet and steer with their hind feet. The sole of the foot has a black dimpled pad to help prevent slipping on the ice.

Can they move quickly?

Although usually slow, polar bears can sprint up to 25 miles (40 km) an hour. They have been known to swim 60 miles (100 km) at a stretch. They can make their way through icy waters for hours at a time.

What about the future?

Polar bears have only one enemy—humans. As well as the danger from hunters, polar bears are threatened with pollution. All across the Arctic, people are moving in to mine oil and coal. Oil spills can be dangerous. Global warming is the greatest threat. If current trends continue in the Arctic, two-thirds of the world's polar bear population could disappear by the year 2050.

Helpful websites:

Polar Bears International
http://www.polarbearsinternational.org/faq/

National Geographic
http://animals.nationalgeographic.com/animals/mammals/polar-bear.html

National Wildlife Federation
http://www.nwf.org/polarbear/

World Wildlife Fund (WWF)
http://www.panda.org/what_we_do/where_we_work/arctic/area/species/polarbear/polar_bear_facts/

PACIFIC OCEAN

NORTH
AMERICA

ARCTIC OCEAN

ASIA

ATLANTIC OCEAN

EUROPE

Polar bear range

INDEX